THE VOLKSWAGEN BEETLE

THE VOLKSWAGEN
BEETLE

Vintage, Restored and Customized

NIGEL GRIMSHAW

INDEX

A SALAMANDER BOOK

Published by Salamander Books Ltd
129-137 York Way
London N7 9LG
United Kingdom

© Salamander Books Ltd, 1995

1 2 3 4 5 6 7 8 9

This edition published in 1996 by
INDEX, Unit 1, Garrard Way,
Kettering NN16 8TD

ISBN 0 86101 903 2

All correspondence concerning the
content of this volume should be
addressed to Salamander Books Ltd.

CREDITS
Managing Editor: Joanna Smith
Editor: Ian Penberthy
Art Editor: Mark Holt
Picture Research: Nigel Grimshaw
Original Design Concept: Aardvark
   Design Studio Ltd
Colour Separation: P & W Graphics
   PTE Ltd
Printed in Italy

CONTENTS

PREFACE 6

HISTORIC BEETLE 8

VINTAGE & RESTORED 14

THE HUMAN CAR 64

BEETLE BEAUTIFUL 90

CONCEPT 1 138

INDEX 142

ACKNOWLEDGMENTS 144

PREFACE

It's difficult to say when I first fell in love with the Beetle. Looking back to my childhood, it probably had something to do with the movies. Not that I want to reveal my age, but back then it was films like *The Italian Job*, with its three Mini Coopers, and of course *Herbie* that formed my image of the car. From this superficial start, the Beetle somehow gained a foothold in my mind, while the Mini Coopers got lost somewhere out on the highway.

Car nuts can be very intense about their own particular obsessions. Whether the object of desire be a Cadillac, Mustang, Mini or Beetle, each group of devotees will tell you that their particular passion is the only one to have - and I am no different. For me, the Beetle is the most enthralling automotive tale ever told. Naturally, all this is subjective, but that is the beauty of concentrating on a certain type of car: it goes deeper - much deeper - than the mechanics of the vehicle; it is a cultural, aesthetic, human and very personal experience. People have been known to lose houses, husbands, wives, girlfriends or boyfriends over their cars, and while I am not advocating that level of commitment, the Beetle does get into your soul, and once there, doesn't let go without a fight.

I'd hazard a guess that this is exactly what happened to the Beetle's inventor, Ferdinand Porsche. Many a car designer would have given up on the Bug when faced with the mountain of problems the project presented in its formative years. But the Beetle got under Porsche's skin, just like it has under mine and that of millions of people like me. He battled through setbacks galore and built arguably the most successful car the world has even seen, in terms of concept, execution and sales.

The Beetle is a car you can't help but fall in love with, which is why I have written this book. It has been put together from the heart to celebrate the Bug in its many wild and wonderful forms. Although it is virtually impossible that all the cars here will appeal to everyone's taste, each has its own unique merits and should be looked at in that light. I have had a ball putting this book together, and I hope you enjoy it as much as I have.

Nigel Grimshaw
Hoddesdon, January 1995

Historic
BEETLE

The Volkswagen Beetle seems to have been with us for all our lives, and for most of us it has. Because the car is such a familiar sight, it is easy to take the Bug's existence for granted, but when you know what it took to put designer Ferdinand Porsche's car into production, you'll be amazed that it ever made it off the drawing board.

The evolution of the Beetle is dotted with milestone dates, and of these 26 May 1938 is one of the most important. This was the day that Adolf Hitler visited the site on which the factory was to be built that would mass-produce the Bug. He was there to lay the first foundation stone, an act that, to all intents and purposes, signified the birth of the Beetle. Of course, years of complex engineering work had led to that famous day, but the laying of that first stone marked the fact that the Bug was a production reality. As well as undertaking his ceremonial duties that day, Hitler also rode in a pre-production Type 38 Cabrio, the car that would become the Beetle we know and love today. Hitler's test drive was a pivotal moment in the Bug's history, signaling the beginning of the most successful car ever built.

Right: The birth of the Beetle went hand-in-hand with the construction of Germany's autobahns. In 1933 Adolf Hitler met the Beetle's designer, Ferdinand Porsche. Hitler knew that Porsche had been working on a small family car, and ordered him to make it ready for production. He then ordered the building of a network of high-speed roads that would act as the infrastructure for Germany's industrial and economic revival.

FERDINAND PORSCHE, designer of the Beetle, built his first car in 1900 for the Viennese coachbuilder Ludwig Lohner. Following his time with Lohner, Porsche moved to Daimler-Benz, and it was while he was with that company that he first hit on the idea of building a small car. This initial design would become the Type 130. Sadly, Daimler-Benz was not as enthusiastic about the 130 as Porsche and, as a result, he was prevented from taking the idea any further. Unhappy at being blocked in this way, but still confident in the idea of a small car, he left Daimler-Benz and headed for Austria to work for Steyr.

Porsche continued working on his ideas for a small car while at Steyr, becoming so confident in his abilities that he decided to set up his own company. To many, however, his timing seemed foolhardy as it coincided with the Wall Street Crash. Nevertheless, Porsche pressed on with his plans by establishing his new company - not in Austria, but in Stuttgart, Germany, where he opened his design office in 1930. Significant as this event was to the Beetle's final success, just two months earlier, a sinister development had taken place when Hitler's National Socialist Workers Party became the second largest political party in Germany.

During the initial period as an independent manufacturer, Porsche attracted a number of outside contracts that kept his business ticking over. However, he was still obsessed with the idea of building a small car, and to this end, established an in-house project running parallel with his other contracts. This initiative was based on the idea of a small, affordable car for the masses, a car that would become known as the Type 12.

At about the same time, the motorcycle firm Zündapp also became interested in the notion of a small car. The company wanted to produce a vehicle that the average person could afford to buy and run, which would be easy to maintain and reliable. Zündapp felt it had identified a lucrative market and wanted to capitalize on it: the company commissioned a rear-engined prototype from Porsche. When finished, the car featured a central-backbone chassis and hinted at what would eventually become the Beetle. However, yet more bad news was on the horizon for Porsche, as on the car's completion Zündapp decided to take the project no further and abandoned the idea. Porsche had to go along with the decision, although he had the foresight to keep the rights to his design.

Next to come to Porsche expressing an interest in the idea of a small, affordable car was NSU, which had Porsche take his ideas a step further by producing the Type 32 prototype. This featured a backbone chassis and rear-mounted, air-cooled engine. Once again, however, the project stumbled to a halt. The problem this time was that NSU was unwilling to provide the funding to put the Type 32 into full production. Without money for tooling and production lines, Porsche's idea came to a standstill once more.

Despite these initial setbacks, another very significant date in the Beetle's evolution loomed. In January 1933, Adolf Hitler came to power in Germany while the world stood back and watched, little knowing what lay in store. Hitler was fascinated by cars and called a meeting with Porsche to discuss ideas for a small, people's car. Outlining his ideas, Hitler emphasized that the car should be capable of carrying two adults and three children, have a maximum speed of 62mph and return 33mpg. Thus commissioned, Porsche went away to design the car, while Hitler put Germany's unemployed to work on building a network of high-speed roads - the autobahns.

Porsche's previous work for both Zündapp and NSU stood him in good stead as he went to work on Hitler's instructions. He was also fortunate in having a strong team of engineers around him.

In June 1934, however, Porsche made one of his worst decisions. He signed a contract

Left: Ferdinand Porsche can arguably be called the most significant car designer in history. His vision of a small family car that was spacious, economical and reliable was inspired. However, putting the Beetle into production was a real struggle, with continual setbacks along the way, although it is notable that these setbacks were rarely due to engineering difficulties. In the main, the problems came from a lack of faith on the part of backers who, having shown initial enthusiasm for the project, backed out when major financial commitment was required. Despite his difficulties, Porsche never gave up on the idea. Surviving various failed partnerships with the likes of Zündapp, Daimler-Benz and NSU, Ferdinand Porsche was always astute enough to retain the rights to his work. This tactic paid off in 1933, when he met with Adolf Hitler and the project became a production reality.

Far left: The launch of the Beetle brought with it jobs for German workers. Initially, these came as Porsche built prototypes to test his ideas and develop his theories, as he worked toward producing the car we know and love as the Beetle. Then, as the car went into production, the number of jobs increased, mushrooming after World War 2 when the Bug began to be exported around the world.

with the German automotive industry (RDA) for the development of the small car project and accepted a down payment. In exchange, he undertook to produce a prototype in just ten months - a ludicrous timescale. Porsche had made a rod for his own back and, to make matters worse, the RDA was not enthusiastic about the project from the start. Needless to say, he did not produce a prototype in the ten months allowed and ended up in hot water with Hitler's government.

During the winter of 1934-5 two Type 60 prototypes were completed, which helped to relieve some of the tension that was beginning to develop between the RDA, the government and Porsche. The Type 60 displayed flowing, aerodynamic lines, inspired by the streamlined race cars of the day, which were very much part of the German approach to automotive design at the time. These flowing lines were beginning to betray the tell-tale shape of the Beetle.

The success of the Type 60 bought Porsche some time, with the deadline being extended by a further 12 months in the name of development. By February 1936 three more prototypes had been built, each having a new 948cc air-cooled, flat-four engine. Rigorous testing was carried out during the fall of 1936, but despite encouraging results, the RDA remained sceptical.

Despite the negative feedback from the RDA, Porsche pressed ahead and, in the spring of 1937, a number of pre-production cars were built, ironically by Daimler-Benz. More than anything that had gone before, these cars had the characteristics, looks and

personality of what would eventually become the Beetle. This was the point at which the appearance of the car was finalized, a look that would remain fundamentally unchanged for 50 years.

Incorporating an oval rear window, a single line of louvers in the metal strip above the engine cover, a one-piece lid at the front and 'frogeye' headlights faired into the fenders, the Beetle was born. This was the Type 38, the car that Hitler took a ride in after laying the foundation stone for the factory that would build the Bug. Wind-tunnel tests showed that Porsche's work on aerodynamics had really paid off: with a cd of just 0.385, the Beetle was both a styling and engineering success.

Another batch of cars was built in 1939, again by Daimler-Benz. Although it was four years since the signing of the original contract, the car was still in prototype form. On the face of it, things were not going well. In addition to the car not being ready for production, there was no factory in which to build it and no dealers to sell it - if and when it was ever produced. However, the decision was made not to sell through dealers, but to use a saving stamp scheme to which potential buyers could subscribe: when they had acquired the appropriate number of credits, they would receive their car. Unfortunately, all this became academic when, in 1939, Germany invaded Poland. Despite the outbreak of World War 2, with the Type 38, Ferdinand Porsche had realized his dream of designing a small, economical family car. The rest, as they say, is history.

Left, below and right: Mass-production techniques were used to meet the demand for Beetles, a demand that grew as markets around the globe fell to the charms of the Bug - although the global appeal of the Beetle did not occur overnight and had to be hard won. Every tactic was used to spread the word about the car, and shows were a major weapon in the sales war. The Beetle would go head-to-head with major manufacturers, including the likes of Cadillac and Ford in the USA. In fact, America proved one of the most difficult territories to crack, the Bug having to create its own alternative culture to win over Americans raised on fins, chrome and V8 engines.

VINTAGE & RESTORED

Where cars are concerned, desirability very often revolves around the notion of rarity. For the uninitiated, however, the idea of a Beetle being rare may seem an odd concept, considering that the Bug sold in larger numbers than even Henry Ford's Model T. But nothing could be further from the truth. To a great extent, the vintage Beetle and restoration scene thrives on the idea of rarity, which stems from the huge variety of specifications produced by VW and the fact that Ferdinand Porsche started work on his ideas for the Beetle back in the late 1920s.

Another factor that has led to the thriving vintage scene is the Bug's phenomenal sales success. Huge numbers of cars were built in the fifties and sixties, and a great many have survived to this day. Because the Bug was built in such vast numbers, there are enough parts in circulation to make restoration a far from impossible task. Even the rarest items can still be found and bought - at a price.

Right: The dream of all car nuts - whether they be into Ferraris, Porsches or Beetles - is an open road, clear skies and enough money for food and gas. These two guys, photographed in the desert north of Los Angeles, have it all. The sky is blue, the road long and empty, and their whitewall-shod oval-window is firing on all cylinders. The Beetle is a state of mind, and it doesn't get any better than this.

WHAT MAKES the vintage Beetle so popular is difficult to determine. In fact, when it was introduced, the Bug was considered an odd-looking little car with, on the face of it, very little potential for world-wide appeal. Yet people fell in love with it and it duly took its place in history. Part of the car's attraction, in vintage form, is undoubtedly its apparent, almost human, personality - it oozes character and charm. These qualities have become even more of a contributory factor in the nineties, as new cars become increasingly similar, antiseptic and downright boring.

There have always been high-quality original Beetles for the simple fact that there have always been people who've bought Bugs new and looked after their cars with a passion. Again, this was a relatively easy thing to do because of the availability of cheap parts and the fact that Beetles are so easy to work on. These were and are the people who simply think that a Beetle is a fun car to own and drive. The arrival of the custom/Cal scene boosted the Beetle's cause and underlined the fact that a Bug was a cool car to own. Then, as the Cal scene developed, people got into building resto-Cals, and soon the vintage Bug got a hold of people's imaginations - the Beetle became a cool car to own in stock or restored form. Of course, many of the cars shown in this chapter cannot truthfully be called stock. Many are what could be called over-restored, with whitewall tires and period accessories well to the fore.

The vintage scene, like customizing, attracts no one particular kind of person, and the cars are as unique as the people who own them. Indeed, many, if not all, of the cars in this chapter have intriguing stories to tell about how they made it this far. One reason for the popularity of the vintage Bug could be its association with the fifties and all the connotations that go with that. The fifties were very positive years, coming after the hardships of World War 2. While it didn't

Left: A Texan goes to Los Angeles: this '57 is a long way from home among the palm trees of Hollywood. Finished in a subtle olive green, this is a cool resto-Cal to the core. There are no extrovert touches, just a subtle lowering job, a period-style roof rack, straight bodywork, and perfect paint.

Far left: This mint '49 Hebmüller is owned by Bob Gilmore, and is one of only 696 such cars produced. It is thought that only 60 still exist. The conversion was carried out by a Ruhr-based coachbuilder. Sadly, the Hebmüller works suffered a serious fire in 1949, and the company never recovered; the model was discontinued in 1950. Bob found the car while on Army service in Germany in 1971.

Above: This '57 oval Deluxe shows that you don't need wild graphic paintwork, trick wheels and an over-the-top interior to produce a great-looking Bug. Virtually stock, apart from the non-original 1200cc engine, it is finished in coral red and rolls on standard wheels, shod with whitewall tires. A ragtop sunroof keeps things cool when temperatures soar, while inside everything is just as it was when the car rolled out of the factory, even down to the stock seats and dashboard.

follow the extravagance of many of the cars that came out of that decade - especially from the American manufacturers - the Beetle represents much of the freewheeling positive feel of that decade. The vintage Beetle represents a simpler, less complicated time, and for many this is all important. What is certainly true about the vintage scene, as it is about most other aspects of owning a Bug, is that it's about lifestyle. Owning a Bug is more than simply owning a means of transport, and the people who restore or run original Beetles buy into a total experience.

Of course, there is more than just emotion involved in owning and restoring a vintage Beetle - there is a practical side too. Restoring a Beetle makes a lot of sense. For a start, the car is relatively easy to work on, with no complicated, computerized engine management systems to get in the way. It also makes financial sense, as a Bug is more likely to hold its value than a new car. Parts are also easy to come by through an infrastructure of suppliers and workshops that exist in almost every country where the Beetle was sold.

As the years roll by and the number of Beetles inevitably dwindles, what constitutes a vintage Bug will change. The day will come when cars from the seventies will be classed as vintage, but not for a long time yet.

Today, the oval- and split-window Bugs fit the bill.

Those outside the Beetle scene may question what it is that attracts people to vintage Bugs - what it is that holds their interest, because once you've seen one restored Bug, you've seen them all, right? Wrong.

VW was constantly changing the Bug's specification, and the fact that the company chose not to equip its cars with very important pieces of kit, such as fuel gauges, meant that companies sprang up offering a huge range of aftermarket parts. These, together with the varying factory specifications, make it possible to build a vintage Bug, using period parts only, that is authentic and unique. Tracking down the parts can become as obsessional as actually building the car, trips to autojumbles, swap meets and shows adding spice to the experience.

People own and restore vintage Beetles for many reasons, but underlying them all is the simple fact that whether it be through looks, its sound or its feel, the car just connects with a great many people on a subconscious level. Some may say that they restore vintage Bugs because they are practical or economical, but when you get right down to it, people just fall in love with the Beetle, and an older car makes for a great alternative.

Left and far left: This junk yard was found in the small town of Hesperia, California, between Los Angeles and Barstow. We happened upon it by chance, at the end of a dirt road, in the middle of nowhere. It's always sad to see any car in a dilapidated condition, but there's something about a classic design, and especially the Beetle, that makes for a captivating image.

Alain Zumofen's '59 Bug has been beautifully restored, and it reflects a time of real change for the Beetle. At the time it was built, VW was developing the Beetle - and fast. The first of the big-window cars came off the production line in 1957, this major change being followed by a number of more minor ones, including alterations to the dashboard, which became easier to read and so more user-friendly. In 1959 VW ceased using semaphore indicators on the Beetle, although US-specification cars lost theirs in 1955. Alain's car is particularly rare in that it has a ragtop sunroof, something that helps his Bug stand out from the crowd in his home country of Switzerland. He aims to keep the car as original as possible, which he has managed to do superbly well so far, even down to the headlight eyebrows and the 30hp motor. The latter has been rebuilt, but carefully to stock specifications.

Englishman Paul Paine bought this '59 Bug in scrap condition and then spent eight hard months restoring it to make a real show-stopper. The car runs a 1600cc twin-port motor with twin Kadron carbs and Quiet Pack exhaust. The transmission is stock. At the rear, the suspension has been lowered two splines, while at the front Sway-Away adjusters have been welded in. Armstrong shocks are used all round. Wheels are standard equipment, but have been stripped, cleaned and repainted. Whitewall tires finish off the rolling stock.

All the body panels are new, while there is a split-window kit at the rear. The interior, including carpeting, seats and headlining, has been retrimmed. The seats have been finished in cream PVC, and there is a matching cream steering wheel. Front headlights are US-specification items, and the heart-shaped rears have been rewired to 12 volts. Accessories include a 1953 Blaupunkt radio and a bud vase.

This car attends many shows, and has won a number of competitions, including Best Vintage, Best resto-Cal and Best Daily Driver.

Randy Ingersoll is the proud owner of this 1950 split-window Beetle. Photographed in the Palm Desert, near Palm Springs, California, this rare sunroof model is one of 12 air-cooled VWs Randy owns; he is the proverbial VW freak. He bought this car from the Indio VW dealership, which had held onto it for 16 years, waiting for the right customer to come along. Apart from the obvious accessories, the car is just as it was the day it rolled out of the factory, back in 1950.

Right: Desert raider: a vintage Cabrio braves the heat of the Californian desert. Although the plate makes it clear that this is no So-Cal creation, this vintage ragtop has been restored to the highest possible standards.

Left & below: This ultra-rare 1952 Beetle Coupe is owned by Englishman Bob Shaill, editor of the *International Vintage VW* magazine. Bob is a VW fanatic through and through; among his previous cars, he can list a 1951 Beetle, a 1949 Hebmüller, four 356 Porsches, a 1972 Karmann Ghia and a 1952 Beetle. Bob bought the Coupe back in 1976 and is the car's fifth owner. It took 14 years to get the Coupe it to its current immaculate condition, and Bob dares not even think how much it has cost to build. Based on the original floorpan, the car is basically as it was in 1952, complete with the original 1131cc engine. The body was built by Karosserie Stoll, a coachbuilder who produced one-off conversions. The two-tone beige paint matches the car's original scheme, while the interior, which seats four, is finished in leather with brown and beige piping.

Left: Robin Allen has owned over 60 cars since 1966, but this 1952 Beetle is his favorite. Bought in April 1970, the car has been on the road constantly, apart from a long lay-off between 1976 and 1990, and has covered a total of 180,000 miles. It still has its original engine, which had a new crankshaft in 1971, and new heads in 1975. It also still has the original transmission, which has needed no major work other than routine servicing. Amazingly, the bodywork has suffered virtually no rust and has never been lifted from the floorpan. The car is the standard German home-market model, hence the lack of chrome.

Above & below: Dave Cantle spotted this 1954 Karmann Cabriolet 20 years ago, when it was still in the possession of its original owner. He knew immediately that this was the car for him, but it took him until 1993 to persuade the owner to sell. The car is the second oldest surviving Karmann Cabriolet in the UK, and is in unrestored condition. Right up to the time he sold it, the original owner used the car as his only form of transport, even taking it on holiday - all the way to the south of France. Dave has no plans to restore his Cabrio, which has an 1198cc engine; he wants to keep it in regular use, just like it's always been.

In 1969 a young German student was on a touring holiday of Europe in his trusty split-window Bug. Eventually, he found himself in London, where Ron Galloway spotted the car parked in the street. Ron had just won some money on a horse race and offered it to the young German for the car. The student accepted and found some other way home to Germany. Ron kept the car for about a year, after which it passed through several pairs of hands before coming to rest with a restorer, who stripped it and stored it for ten long years. Then, during the winter of 1988, Karl Metcalfe was desperately looking for a good split-window when he came across the car. It was love at first sight, so he bought the car there and then. After a detailed restoration job, the Bug is now back on the road in fine form.

Above & left: A right-hand-drive 1954 oval-window is rare indeed, especially in original showroom condition. Alf Lilley, of Stoke-on-Trent, England, is the owner, who says the only work he's done on the car is to clean it. This seems impossible, given that it has spent its life in rainy England. However, the original owner looked after it meticulously and never drove it in the rain. It was used like this until 1972, when it was put into storage. Accessories include Robri gravel guards, a hood handle guard and headlight eyebrows.

Right: A classic cream oval-window. Subtle modifications and a lot of hard restoration work have gone into making it a real eye-catcher. The bodywork is perfect, as is the paint, while the suspension has been tweaked a little for a more purposeful stance. The chrome has been renewed and whitewalls have been added to give it that authentic resto-Cal feel.

Little is known about this '54 oval-window, except that until 1990, it had only covered 60,000 miles. In that year it was offered to a motor museum, but was rejected because there was already an example in the collection. At this point, John Deveraux came into the picture. He was looking for an oval-window for his girlfriend, and the '54 was ideal. When he bought the Bug, it was far from perfect, but it had been stripped for restoration. The body was removed from the chassis and taken back to bare metal, while the floorpan was sandblasted clean. Anything that needed replacing was renewed, but the bodywork was excellent and needed little attention. The interior was retrimmed to finish the job.

This Jungle Green '54 Export-Deluxe is owned by British based Brett Moxom. The car has been completely restored with much care being taken to keep it as original as possible. During the restoration, the body was removed to ensure that the floorpan was in good shape, and new panels were fitted, including inner fenders, fenders, and front and rear valances. The seats, door panels and sunroof were all recovered, while the engine - a 25hp, 1131cc unit - was stripped and cleaned. Brett drives his '54 as often as he can and has won a number of trophies with the car, but he says he's more interested in having fun with it than winning silverware. He has owned four Beetles in total, starting with a '73, and then a '72 1302S before moving onto a '64. This oval-window is the last of the line, being the car he's always wanted.

Not even a rainy day can dull the effect of this superbly restored '54 Cabrio. Although the weather means that the top does not come down as often as it would in California, owner Howard Chadwick still uses the car as often as he can. The car runs a 30hp engine, which has been stripped and cleaned, but still features stock internals. The interior has been retrimmed in line

with the original specification, as has the top. Howard used many new-old-stock parts to finish the car, including fanfare horns, Bosch spotlights, badge bar bug deflector, Robri gravel guards, Hella fan and Hella dash spotlight. It also has high-speed wipers, a Moto Meter rally dash, trip speedo and Petri steering wheel with horn ring and sundial horn push.

Nick Britten is the owner of this immaculate 1955 Cabrio. The car is one of the most famous open-top Bugs in the UK, having been restored originally by Ritchie King, over a seven year period. The '55 runs a 1771cc engine with EMPI quick-shift box and, according to Nick, 'goes like stink.' At the moment, the Cabrio is used purely as a show car and is kept in dry storage throughout the winter, safe from the ravages of damp winter weather. It features just about every option under the sun, with the combination of a powerful engine and cross-ply tires making driving a very hairy experience!

This super '57 Bug is owned by Jean-Michel Schiettecatte, who runs a high-class restaurant in London. As a rule, he parks his car outside the entrance, where it is usually surrounded by Ferraris, BMWs and Jaguars. Yet no matter how many supercars there are, the Bug always receives the most attention. It runs its original 1200cc engine and has been resprayed polar silver. Interior accessories include a parcel shelf, bud vase, St Christopher badge, glove box handle and passenger grab handle; outside there are Robri stone guards and chrome wheel trims.

This resto-Cal was bought as an abandoned project in 1990 by current owner Stuart Groce, who took eight months to complete the slammed '57. The car was bought with the proceeds from the sale of Stuart's previous Bug, as were all the necessary parts. It has been lowered two splines at the rear, and has had Sway-Aways welded in at the front. All the bodywork, including preparation and flatting, was carried out by Stuart, although the final top coat was trusted to a professional spray shop. Inside, the seats, steering wheel and gauges are standard, but an aftermarket stereo has been fitted.

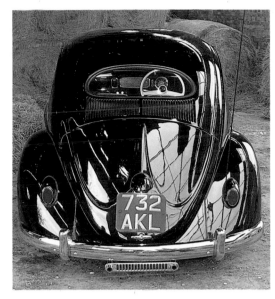

Robin Allen spotted this '57 in the British magazine *Auto Trader*. When he arrived to look at the car, it didn't seem too promising. It had been hand painted, the chrome was red with corrosion, and the interior looked like it had been attacked by moths. On closer inspection, however, Robin realized that the car was actually quite solid; it also had its original 1192cc engine. After due consideration, he bought the car. Initially, he was going to use it as a runabout, but when the crankshaft snapped he decided on a full, concours restoration. The car was stripped to bare metal, confirming that it was in fine condition. It was then painted horizon blue, with two-tone wheels. The engine was stripped, cleaned and rebuilt to its original specification. Inside, a new headliner was sourced, the seats recovered and new carpets made - also to the original specification. All parts used were either new-old-stock or sound originals. With some carefully chosen period accessories - like whitewall tires, dual-mounted radio aerial and headlight eyebrows - the result was one fine '57.

Swiss national Fournier Gilbert bought this '58 Bug in 1988, rescuing it from a barn where it had been in storage. It was in great shape despite having stood idle for several years, and after a three-month restoration was ready for the road. The car was sprayed metallic beige (an authentic VW color), the chrome was replaced, and the bodywork and floorpan checked for rot - none was found. Since completion, it has attended events throughout Europe. When asked about his car, Fournier said: 'The Beetle is not only a car, but a way of life, a reason to drive. A car that is in your heart.'

A Beetle from the land of the Beatles. Philip Briscoe, owner of this spotless '59 Karmann convertible, is a native of Liverpool, England. This two-tone black and cream drop-top has been restored to tip-top health from stem to stern. The engine is a stock 1200cc unit, which has been stripped and cleaned, while all the chromework has been refinished. The interior, including seats, carpet and door panels, has been completely retrimmed, and the stock steering wheel has been retained. Accessories have been kept to a minimum, but there is a bud vase, a six-volt fan and a parcel shelf. The car has been fitted with a new top, while whitewall tires round off the whole deal. Philip uses the convertible as often as he can, when the weather allows, and he also hires it out as a wedding car for Beetle-crazy couples.

Belgium is a hotbed of top-class Bugs, and they don't come any better than Danny Herman's '61 Cabrio. This car has had a phenomenal amount of care and attention lavished upon it. Danny's aim was to keep it as close to its original specification as possible, hence the 34hp 1192cc engine, single-circuit brakes, synchromesh transmission and six-volt electrical system. While the car has been resprayed, much remains unrestored, and is all the more interesting for it. The interior still features the original seats, which have not been re-upholstered, and while they do show signs of wear, this adds to the overall attraction of the car.

In 1961 Beetles lacked many useful items, and there was a strong demand for aftermarket equipment. In keeping with this, Danny's car features accessories such as a Dehne fuel gauge, rear fog light, fire extinguisher and Bambus parcel shelf. To maintain the original theme, the Bug still rolls on cross-ply tires, while the engine compartment, though clean, shows signs that this car is used on a regular basis and is not kept locked away for posterity.

In Switzerland, back in 1963, most head postmasters drove specially-adapted Beetles. Unfortunately, most of these cars have been scrapped, but Martial Oberon's Bug escaped the crusher. Martial is only the second owner of this '63, which is said to have been used solely to deliver telegrams, and then only when the weather was bad. When it fell into Martial's hands, the Beetle was in a bad way, but it had just 70,000km on the clock plus a factory ragtop sunroof.

There was never any question in Martial's mind that he would buy the car, nor was there ever any doubt that he would restore it to its original Post Office specification. The car still features many accessories used by the Post Office, including an Eberspacher BN2 gas heater, roof and boot racks, a gear-stick lock and a full first aid kit. The interior is also awash with goodies, including a Becker quick-release radio and a very rare ashtray light.

Owned by Maurey Cole, of Huntington Beach, California, this Hebmüller has been fully restored and is finished in chocolate brown. It features a brown and beige interior, which is set off by a tan top. Power comes from an Okrasa engine, which makes this already rare car, with its distinctive license plate, even more of a stand-out.

When Welshman Robert Wynne bought this car, it was completely rotten. From floorpan to decklid, the dreaded rust had done its worst. Because of its poor state, Robert managed to buy the car for a song, but it took a lot more cash and over four years to get it running again. All the mechanical work was done by the owner, which is a great testimony to his skill and determination, as he is neither a mechanic nor a bodyman by trade. Finished in ruby red, the '64 Cabrio features a 1200cc engine, which has been checked and given a clean bill of health. The interior has been retrimmed to complement the rest of the car, while the top is also new.

Belgian Mon Martens' amazing Type 151 is the result of a two-year restoration job. The car left the factory, in Osnabrück, on 16 September, 1960, and was delivered to a dealer in Essen. By way of a number of owners, it eventually fell into Mon's caring hands. It is virtually impossible to criticize anything about this car; it is as near as possible exactly the same as the day it left the factory. The body color is the same pearl white, as are all the other painted items, such as the steering wheel. The car has also been fitted with a large number of period accessories

to enhance its looks, including very rare Robri running-board step plates with matching gravel guards for the fenders. There are Foxcraft fender skirts, Cabrio decklid vent trims and much sought-after Lemmertz beauty rings. The bumpers are also a little different, being optional US export items. Inside, there is a Dehne fuel gauge, a steering/ignition lock and a period radio. The engine has been fully renovated, the only non-original part being a Fram bypass oil filter, but that was a factory accessory, so it could have been fitted when the car was built.

Above: What could be finer than cruising the freeway in an open-topped Bug? The sun sits high in the sky, the radio sounds fine, and everything is right with the world. The simple joy of wind-in-the-hair driving, to the accompaniment of a purring flat-four, air-cooled engine, is rich indeed.

Right: No matter from what angle you view a vintage Beetle, it looks fantastic. This resto-Cal oval-window, with its period suitcase and rack, looks the business parked on the street in Los Angeles. It is in great shape and ready to give many years of stylish service.

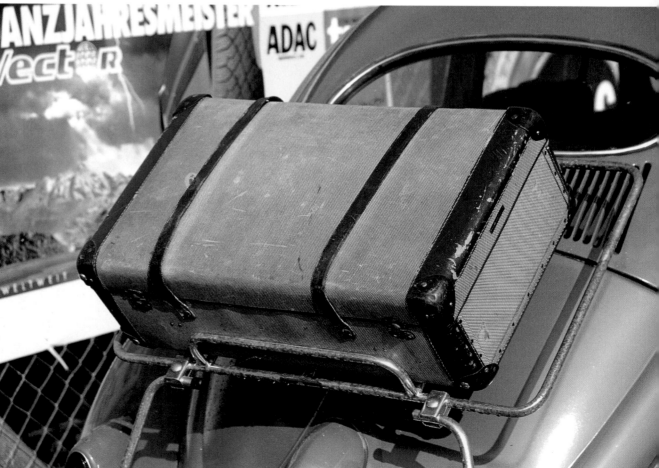

Left & below: The world never looks better than through the windows of a vintage Bug. Whether it be a split-window, oval-window or later model, this is a great way to see life - especially if the sun's shining and the palm trees are swaying gently.

THE HUMAN CAR

Beetles are about the people who own them, and for every car - whether it be a stocker, custom or racer - there is usually a story to tell. While researching this book, I met many hundreds of Beetle enthusiasts and spent many a happy hour listening to stories about their Bugs. And each story is as individual as the person telling it.

Far from being boring, the human aspect of the Beetle story is one you can never tire of hearing. The tales of life with Beetles are as rich and varied as the cars themselves.

Right: Beetles have become synonymous with youth culture, and especially the surf scene. Now whether or not this has something to do with the fact that Californians were the first to start personalizing their Bugs, and were the same people to develop the definitive Cal-look is unclear, but Beetles and surfing go together like sun and fun. And there's no point in fighting it; all you can do is sling your boards in the back, pick up your buddies, and head for the beach.

ONE GIRL I met had been saving up to buy a Bug since she was ten and had just taken delivery of a fully restored '67 model - she had just turned 17 and had passed her driving test on the previous day. Then there was the guy who tracked down an original, unrestored split-window, still in the hands of its original German owners. He managed to buy the car and drove it back home to England, where it was rebuilt. He then drove the Bug back to Germany to show the original owners his handiwork. They were so impressed at seeing 'their' car in such fine condition that they burst into tears - of joy.

And finally, there was the manager of a high-class restaurant in London's West End, who parked his oval-window outside the restaurant every day. Among his clientele were Cindy Crawford, Richard Gere and Princess Diana, but no matter how many Ferraris, Rolls Royces or Lamborghinis were parked near his Bug, it was always the Beetle that drew the biggest crowd. He'd lost count of the number of offers he'd had from wealthy customers wanting to buy it.

To get a real impression of what being into Beetles is all about, the best place to visit is a show. Whether they are small, single-day events or massive weekenders, Beetle shows are renowned for being among the best car shows in the world.

If you are not a regular VW show-goer already, don't be misled into thinking that these events are similar to other kinds of car show, with much car polishing and jostling for the top trophies. While trophy winning is a part of Beetle events, it is far from the be-all-and-end-all. Bug shows are a full-on experience for the senses - an all-out assault of color, noise and fun. They are also great places to see what all the other Beetle builders are up to: what the new colors and styles are, who's doing what, what's in and what's not. Shows are also great places to go parts hunting, with many traders and Beetle enthusiasts taking

Left and far left: Regardless of what kind of Beetle freak you are, shows are great places to check out the latest trends and see what other VW fans are doing. Far from being stuffy affairs, as is often the case with other kinds of car show, Beetle happenings are free-flow events where almost anything goes. You'll get any and every kind of Bug entering, and 'Vanishing Point' is a good example. An alternative Baja Bug, it has wheels that certainly aren't as over-the-top as you'd see on many race cars, while the paint certainly hasn't seen a desert race track in a long time - judging by the immaculate finish. Plenty of spit and polish have gone into making sure that 'Vanishing Point' has every chance of winning an award. And the guy in the shades? Why, he's one of the judges of course!

the opportunity to sell and swap parts and accessories.

Beetle shows take place all around the world, but whether it be in southern California, Europe or anywhere else, the sights and sounds remain the same. Funfairs, show 'n' shines, bikini competitions - you name it, all life is there. Of course, the cars are the center of attention, with stockers, vintage, customs and racers all mixing at the same events.

And if you talk to people who exhibit their cars at VW shows, you'll often hear crazy tales of many sleepless nights spent in workshops, rushing to get cars ready in time. The competition to have the coolest, most radical car on the block is intense.

Of course, it's not only shows where you get to see Beetles in action - the world's race tracks also offer the opportunity to see outrageous Bugs. Beetle people are into all kinds of motorsport, from small-time circuit racing to land speed record attempts at Bonneville. The world of Beetle racing is as colorful and as exciting as the shows themselves - the sight of a drag race Bug with its wheels pointed skyward, launching hard off the line is difficult to beat, at any sort of race meeting.

If you spend any time at all around Beetles, one thing becomes apparent very quickly: the cars and the people are inseparable. Like no other car before, and no other car since, the Beetle has a human aspect. Human in the sense that each car has a personality in the way it draws an emotional response from its owner. Other groups of car owners will say that they love their cars, which I am sure is true, but not in the sheer numbers this car can boast - the VW Beetle is a legitimate phenomenon.

The commitment of the people to their cars is as fervent as you'll find anywhere. In fact, it is this commitment that, to a great degree, marks out Beetle people. You'll find them in almost every country of the motoring world. They are members of a world-wide movement that seems to be self-perpetuating, even though the car itself has been out of production in the West for many years.

Clichés aren't always apt, but as far as Beetle events are concerned, it is a fact that a picture is worth a thousand words. No way can anyone properly describe the sights and sounds of a good Bug show. The best thing to do is just look at the pictures, imagine that the sun is beating down and that you're surrounded by row after row of the best-looking Bugs around. If you're lucky, when you open your eyes, it might even be true.

Left: It's not only the cars that have to be elaborately prepared for a show. Such is the high standard of show Bugs that owners have to make an extra effort to ensure that their cars stand out from the crowd. One of the best ways of doing this is to build a display set. Here we have a typical beach scene, complete with palm trees, sand and a beach ball, to complement a great-looking peach and white Cal-looker.

Beetles can become an obsession. First, the cars themselves are the attraction, so you learn to drive and buy your first Bug. Then you buy a more expensive Beetle, and from there you may get into customizing or racing, or maybe buy yourself a vintage Bug and start restoring and' collecting rare parts. Then there is all the paraphernalia that surrounds the Beetle legend: the magazines, the books, the T-shirts and the toys. Here we have just a small selection of what can be collected. At far left is one of many different T-shirts. To the right is a collection of model Bugs, one bearing the EMPI logo, while below is a more gimmicky approach, with cartoon-like models sporting V8 motors and superchargers.

Say it loud, and say it proud! It can never be said that the Beetle hasn't plenty to say for itself. This outspoken character probably derives from the fact that very few Bugs are ever alike. Ever since the car went into production, the Volkswagen factory continuously changed the specifications, and this was before the aftermarket accessory companies started confusing matters even further. However, if a Beetle owner wants to shout a little louder still, there's a whole range of special plates available to put the message across in true Beetle style. Whether it be shouting about home town Wolfsburg, or saying it loud and proud for the vintage Bug, Beetle owners like to be seen, heard and read.

License plates are almost an art form in the United States, and none more so than among Beetle owners. This collection of plates just about says it all, from the vintage style of 'MY 49 VW' to the attitude of 'LO PEACH' - the Bug has more to say for itself than just about any other car. And even though this is a fairly random selection, most of these cars turn out to be from California, home of the most radical Bugs and, it would seem, the most radical plates.

Left: Standing back to admire his handiwork is the owner of this clean '63 Cal-looker. Taking your own car to a show, a car you built yourself, can be one of the most gratifying feelings around. This guy certainly seems to think so, and to such an extent that he's made his own T-shirt to commemorate the occasion. And who can blame him? He's built a straight-looking car with polished alloys, clean paint, and an arrow straight body. With all this hard work in the bag, maybe, just maybe, someone will see fit to give him a trophy...here's hoping.

Below: While some people spend thousands on their cars, others take a different route. This Bug won't win any Best of Show trophies and it will probably be a while before it sees a car wash, but somehow that doesn't matter. Other cars looking like this would come across as sad and neglected, but the Beetle just oozes more character. Of course, it could be the anti-nuclear graffiti, the smily face and the LOVE logo that does it...a hippy trip to the sixties. Or it could be the Californian plates and the fact that Californians seem able to make Beetles look good no matter what.

Beetles come in many styles, which is clearly demonstrated by these two cars. Below is an original split-window with a load of period parts for sale, while to the right is an altogether more potent proposition. To many, shoehorning a V8, especially a Hemi V8, into a Bug is sacrilege. But you have to hand it to this guy, whether you like the idea or not. The standard of workmanship is superb. And he's got it right with the name - 'Herbie on Steroids'. The Hemi engine was, and still is, a potent piece of equipment. In a straight line, this car must take some beating, but negotiating a bend with all that weight in the front must be an interesting experience.

FirePower

HERBIE ON STEROID's
392 HEMI
MUSTANG II FRONT
FRAME: FAST TRACK
ROGERS

Left: A typical display for an LA Bug. The radical top and black paint demonstrate why this Bug is so successful on the show circuit - check out the trophies scattered around the display.

Right: Many small businesses have grown up to supply owners with pictures and hand-painted T-shirts depicting their cars. The artists concerned are often very talented. Witness this guy, whose vivid use of color and interpretative style make for a great T-shirt. Many of these artists can be found at shows throughout the summer months.

Below: Even VW accessory shops are cool. The comic logo sums up the kind of customer this shop owner is trying to attract.

Baja racing is great to watch, and it also makes for one of the most photogenic of all VW events. Out in the desert, miles from anywhere, it's man and machine against the terrain and elements. All you can do is prepare the car as well as possible, then go for broke. And if the car does really does 'go for broke', then stand back and watch the rest race by…just like these guys are doing.

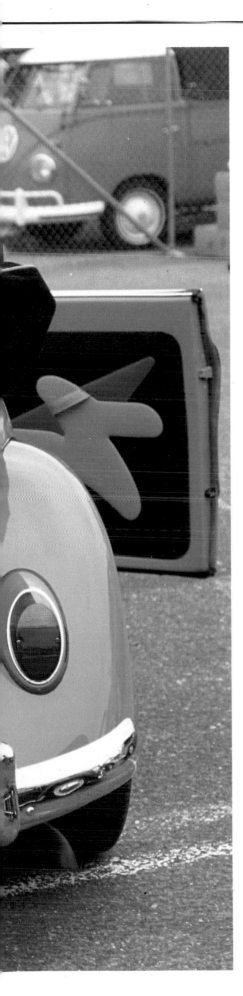

Left: It's all in the detail. A highly-polished engine uses innovative design and styling to set the car apart from the crowd, while a set of wild door panels reinforces the point the owner is trying to make. Employing these sorts of tricks can turn an impressive but average Cal-looker into a show stopping winner.

Right: Beetle owners have a sense of humor…they need it. Many of the uninitiated find it difficult to understand the attraction of the Bug, but enough people know that if you have to ask why, you'll never understand the answer. And as the sign quite rightly points out, 'Old VWs don't drop oil, they just mark their spot'.

Below: I'm not sure whether this Bug was ever actually used as a cab, but it sure looks like a great idea. A checkered paint job and some interesting accessories, including eyebrows and whitewall tires, add up to an authentic-looking Beetle taxi. As for that thing attached to the window; would you believe it's an air conditioner?

Left: All kinds of Bugs turn up to shows. A classic line-up of vintage Ovals basks in the afternoon sun. Whether they are accessorized like the luggage carrying car in the foreground or running virtually stock, a row of Ovals will certainly bring out the best in any show.

Above right: Time to go. The show's over and out comes the hand crank for the drive home. I just hope he can get the thing started and makes it home after the show closes.

Below right: A cool Cal-looker kicks back in the heat. Polished alloys, monotone paint and a ragtop make this one subtle beach cruiser.

'Billabug' was designed and built in England. Inspired by the Australian surf scene and, more incredibly, by a pair of shorts from the Billabug clothing company, the car was built to be subtle outside, but totally over-the-top inside. The subtle approach belies the amount of work that has gone into this '64, which includes a pillarless conversion, deseaming, and extended rocker panels and fenders. The rear vents incorporate a wave design, while the early solid wheels are cut with directional teardrop motifs. The doors are solenoid operated, and the fenders have hidden mountings. 'Billabug' is one of the most famous Cal-lookers in England, and was one of the first Beetles to forge a link between VWs and the surf scene in the UK.

Beetle
BEAUTIFUL

It seems that people have been customizing the Beetle virtually since it went into production. In fact, you can trace modified Beetles back as far as 1956, when the American EMPI company began producing tuning equipment for the Bug. Although 1956 may seem a long way off, the influence of those early cars can still be felt in the nineties, with many modified cars today following the style of those early cars.

California was the birthplace of the customized Beetle, but it didn't take long for the West Coast phenomenon to spread across the world. Today, custom Bugs can be found in virtually every country where the Beetle was ever sold.

Right: 'Outrage Us' belongs to Englishwoman Jan Deal. Jan forms part of the crew of the 'Outrage' Beetle funny car. Fed up with watching from the wings, Jan decided to have a go at drag racing herself. The result is this street 'n' strip Bug. Modifications include a 5in roof chop, lowered suspension and a 1776cc motor running Mahle pistons, Eurorace rods, Scat camshaft and twin carbs. On its first outing, the car covered the quarter mile in 15.99 seconds.

THE MOST popular custom Bug is the Cal-looker. As the name suggests, Cal-look began in California where it was first recognized in the mid-seventies. The roots of the style lie very much with early drag race cars, highlighting the link between customizing, racing and street performance. Many of the early VW clubs formed in California, like Der Kleiner Panzers, were performance orientated: the drag strip refugee look of lowered front end, roll cage and hot engine was, and in many cases still is, the hot ticket.

Cal-look is successful for a great number of reasons, not least of which is that it is one of the easiest conversions to carry out, and one of the least expensive. Having said that, the only limitation is the builder's imagination, with any number of variations finding their place in the basic style. Roof chops, targa roofs and suicide doors all contribute to Cal-look - and much more besides.

Within the confines of Cal-look, builders can be as subtle or as outrageous as they like.

Wild graphic paint jobs, highly polished alloy wheels and extreme interiors are as acceptable as more subtle stock interiors, standard wheels and monotone paint.

There are many theories as to why Cal-look is so popular. One is that it remains faithful to the Beetle's origins. However, this loyalty to the original car's looks is exactly why some people go for more outrageous approaches - the Cal-look is simply not wild enough for these folk.

The most obvious alternative to Cal-look is Baja. Rather than staying faithful to the original tin and going for a smooth, low approach, Baja is a much more aggressive style and is less faithful to the Bug's origins. Baja takes its name from the Baja peninsula in California, home to some of the most spectacular off-road racing in the world. As you would expect, the Baja Bug steers clear of everything that is Cal-look and goes for a tough, hiked-up, off-road stance with bobbed fenders and super-strong running gear. But the

Below left: A cool Cal-looker where it belongs, down at the beach. Low stance, graphic paint and a roof rack for the surf boards make this a classic example and no mistake.

Right: Switch the scene to Europe and this deep blue show winner. Running a 1598cc engine, this '56 oval-window has collected eight Best of Show trophies on Britain's vibrant show scene.

Below: A Baja Bug returning home after a day spent doing what comes naturally. Contrast is the name of the game where the Beetle is concerned and the three examples here couldn't be more different.

Baja is far from just an off-road bruiser; like the Cal-looker, it also finds a home on the street and at the beach. There are also more than enough chromed-up Baja show queens to match the best of Cal-look.

As with Cal-look, there are many different ways of building a Baja Bug. Within the essential ingredients of raised suspension, big chunky tires and chopped fenders, there is scope for mild or wild paint, hot race-bred engines or more practical and streetable units. Interiors are clean and functional, with tough-looking roll cages and mega-watt stereos all on the menu.

Cal-look and Baja, while very popular, don't account for the whole of the Volkswagen customizing scene. Over the years, Beetles have been built as V8-powered Pro-Streeters, hydraulically suspended Low Riders or even pretend fifties-style hot rods. As strange or ridiculous as some of these creations may sound, most of them do turn out to be real winners.

Not all customized or modified Beetles are built for the street or shows: there is one other area where Bugs make a really big impact - racing. We've already looked at the Baja, which covers the off-road angle, but there is far more to Beetle racing than just thrashing about in the dirt. Bugs crop up in many areas of motorsport, and are successful with it. From the drag strips of the USA to the circuits of Europe, Beetles can be found competing hard and winning.

Left: A drag race Bug looks like a real contender. Rear aerodynamic mods are designed to keep the power on the track, while the parachute hints that this is no average race car.

Right: What can you say about this? Many believe that the Beetle is an artform, but surely this is taking matters a little too far.

Below: A cool Cabrio pulls out into the traffic. Whether on the street or the track, the Beetle is one of the most photogenic cars ever built.

On the face of it, the Beetle may not seem like the perfect race car, but it is a very able competitor, never more so than on the world's drag strips. Because of its rear-engined layout, the Bug is well suited to putting huge amounts of power down on the ground, as the weight of the engine sits over the driving wheels. After all, if you're going to install an expensive, high-power engine, there is no point in having all that grunt go up in smoke because of wheelspin. Indeed, many a big V8 racer has been surprised by a Bug blasting past to cross the finish line first.

A typical drag race Bug combines a powerful engine with light GRP panels, all based on a stock floorpan. However, the quicker the car, the more likely it is to have a full tube chassis, roll cage and braking parachute. There is a lot of expense involved in building a competition Beetle, but above and beyond the cost - and the danger - associated with building quick and competitive cars, Beetle racing is all about taking part and having some fun.

At the end of the day, one thing separates the Beetle customizing and racing enthusiasts from the rest, and that is their innovation and appetite for change. There are professional bodyshops and talented individuals, working from home, in countries all around the world, honing their cars and dreaming up new and innovative ways of doing things. An infrastructure of parts suppliers and workshops provides the builders with a supply of raw materials, while several Beetle-orientated magazines keep everyone up to date with the latest trends.

One thing is for sure: as long as there are Beetles, they will always be modified.

John Humphreys, owner of this 1954 oval-window, certainly went to town when he decided to build his own Cal-looker. He was determined that everything should be done right, so the whole car was stripped to ensure that anything that was decayed or broken could be repaired or replaced. The car runs a 1600cc engine with standard crank, rods, cam, pistons and cylinder heads. Twin Dellorto carbs feed the fuel, while a dual Quiet Pack exhaust makes sure the gases escape in the correct manner. The suspension has been lowered front and rear, and heavy-duty shocks are used to iron out the bumps. The gearbox is a standard 1300 unit, while there are drum brakes front and rear. During the rebuild, the body was separated from the floorpan and the underpinnings shotblasted, zinc plated and color matched to the rest of the car. EMPI-style five-spoke wheels carry Dunlop rubber, which provides plenty of grip. Inside, the car features red leather upholstery and Wilton carpets - the seats are Recaro at the front and standard Beetle in the rear. The entire interior has been color coded to match the red leather of the upholstery.

Englishman Brian Burrows had always fancied owning the only VW Beetle funny car in the UK, so he set out to build one. He contacted Creative Car Craft in Florida, USA, a company that makes stretched, one-piece Bug bodies. Creative Car Craft agreed to build Brian a body that would be lighter than regular fiberglass, by using glass cloth rather than mat. The body is 16in longer than the standard Beetle, and the roof has been chopped 4in. Once the body was under way, Brian went ahead and ordered an engine from Autocraft Engine of Ohio. What he actually bought was a 2.8-liter, turbocharged flat-four that pushes out 682bhp and 512lb/ft of torque. The engine runs on methanol, features a dry sump, and drives through a Powerglide automatic transmission equipped with an electronic shift change and trans brake. After some initial testing, the car now runs straight and true, turning in a number of record-breaking times. The car also competes at static events around Europe and is a crowd favorite everywhere it appears.

When Mark Williams bought this '56 oval-window Cal-looker, it had already been partially restored, so he set about finishing the job. First, he added blade fenders and chrome mirrors to complement the small amount of chrome that remained. A header system and stainless single Quiet Pack exhaust were fitted, along with Eagle 520 wheels and detailed brakes. Mark stripped, cleaned and detailed the engine, which now features twin Kadrons, chrome louvered firewall, chrome tinware, chrome generator cover and fuel pump. All the carb linkages were sprayed to match the body color, while tube coverings were made for the HT leads. The front seats were replaced, but the rear one remained, having been reupholstered; the door panels were supplied by Sewfine. The speedo was removed, stripped and color coded, while the car was fully alarmed and has a sound system designed and installed by Mark himself.

Left: There's no doubting the message here. This little green Bug means business.

Right: 'Shutterbug' is owned by photographer and veteran drag racer Jim Kelso. This picture was taken at the Firebird International Raceway in Arizona, at the start of another hard-charging, eight-second run. 'Shutterbug' features a stretched, narrowed and chopped fiberglass body, while power comes from a 461ci big-block Chevy that puts out 500bhp through a Powerglide transmission.

Below: Let it all hang out: this Baja back end hasn't seen a desert race track for a few years.

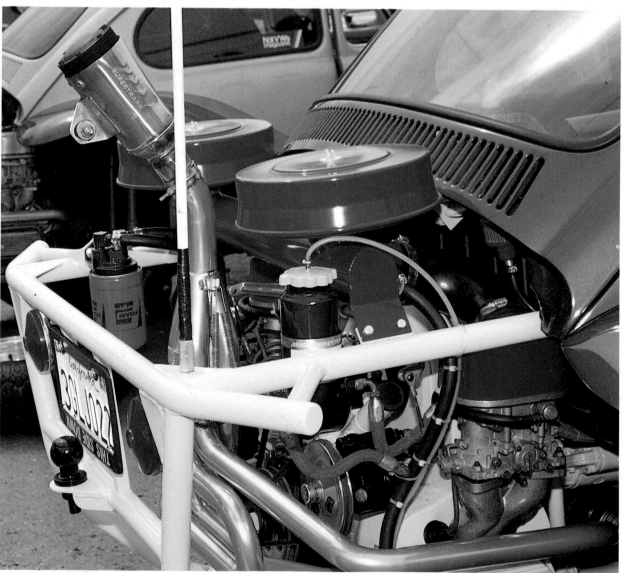

Lars Holmer comes from Denmark, which is well known for its high-class Cal-lookers. His car, a 1951 Type 1, runs an 1835cc engine with Dellorto carbs and electronic ignition, while a 1200 transmission passes the power to the wheels. Sway-Aways have been welded into the front suspension, and the rear suspension has been lowered two splines. Koni shocks have been used all round. Notably, the transmission has been raised ⅝in (15mm) to aid ground clearance. The body has been dechromed and painted in a custom-mixed blue, set off by Porsche five-spoke wheels all round. The front lights have US specification indicators, while the rears have heart-shaped lenses. Inside, the seats have been recovered in leather, and there is a new headliner and carpet. In addition, there are rechromed fenders, a billet mirror, billet fender irons, detailed suspension, billet bonnet hinges, aluminum fuel tank, tinted glass and a Kenwood sound system with CD.

Trevor Chennells' Beetle roadster took two years to build and is based on a 1970 floorpan, which is the only part of the original car that remains. The 1835cc engine is from a '73 Beetle and features Eliminator heads, although the carbs are standard due to a lack of space, but Trevor is working on a solution for this. The car has an estimated top speed of 115mph and returns about 28mpg. Transmission is through a standard manual box with a quick shifter, while the rear has been lowered 3in, and the front one spline. Wheels are 16in Porsche Fusch alloys, running 45-series tires. The most striking aspect of this car is the bodywork. Trevor fitted the roadster kit himself, adding frenched tail-lights, a Testarossa side pod kit, Ford Escort RS Turbo hood louvers and modified side skirts. The doors are solenoid-operated, while the body is finished in Ford metallic Apollo Green paint.

The interior has been trimmed in leather, complemented by Wilton carpets, and there is an aluminum-topped roll bar. A folding mohair top keeps the rain off if the British weather decides to do its worst.

Competition Beetles come in all shapes and sizes. There are circuit racers, drag racers, and there are Baja Bugs. Born out of off-road racing, Baja Bugs are among the most exciting of all competition Beetles. The four cars pictured here were photographed during a race in the desert, but Baja Bugs can also be found on the street, or taking part in shows, where they can be as glitzy as any other top-class trophy hunters.

Baja Bugs are often run by people who want an alternative to the Cal-look. Consequently, they favor raised suspension and a much more rugged look. The fact that many Baja Bugs are raced in the exacting conditions of the desert means that the cars are built to a very high standard, and while they are obviously tough, the same attention is paid to the finish with exceptional paint jobs. Which all adds up to cars that look as tough as they run.

As with many car projects, the evolution of Mark Bailey's stock '71 sedan to a tricked-out roadster has been long and sometimes painful. Mark bought the car in 1988, and soon after he decided that he could not live with a stocker and Cal-look was the only way to go. So the car was taken to the Paintbox bodyshop, where some months later it reappeared as a slammed, lilac Cal-looker. Mark ran the car like this for a few years before he suddenly got a yearning for a roadster. Again he approached the Paintbox who agreed to do the work. The roof was removed and a 2in box-section was steel welded around the floor-pan to replace the lost strength. Steel tubing was also set into the windshield posts and door areas for rigidity. The rear section of the body was then painstakingly grafted in, while hidden hinges were fitted and the door handles removed. Porsche wheels were then fitted, and the whole car was carefully repainted and retrimmed. All this added up to a lot of time and hard work, but the end result is a great looking car to be proud of and a trophy winner into the bargain.

Many drag racers think that the Beetle is a joke, but they often get a nasty surprise on the strip when they are blown away by the same Bug they were joking about. In fact, the Bug is well equipped for drag racing. Having the engine over the rear wheels aids weight transfer, so that the power is put down on the tarmac where it belongs. This often leads to spectacular wheelstands, as demonstrated by British racer Keith Seume in his championship-winning car.

Typically, a drag race Bug uses a stock floorpan and a hot engine. However, in the more potent machines it is not uncommon to find tube frames, full roll cages and braking parachutes being used to make sure they get to the end of the track safely. From the low-cost street classes to the quickest competition cars, the root of Beetle drag racing lies in having fun.

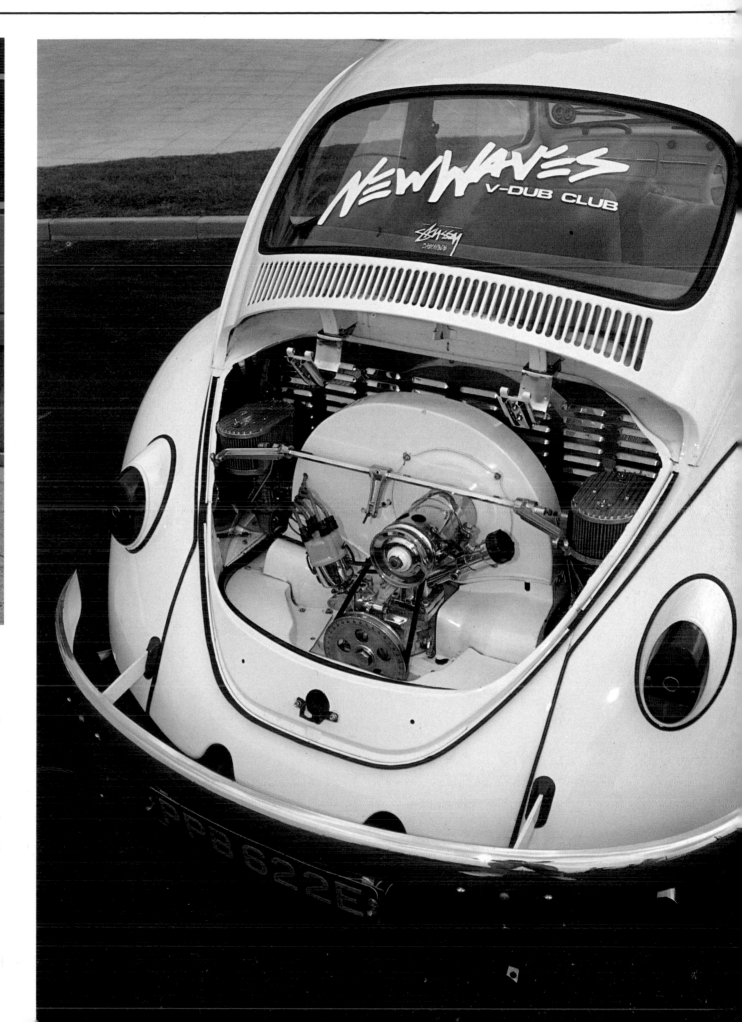

Classic Cal style from Howard Blenkiron's Bug. Beginning with a stock '67 sedan, the first job was to ensure that the body and floorpan were free from rot. Then the engine was overhauled. The 1600cc flat-four features twin-port heads and twin baby Dellorto carbs, while the exhaust is a twin Quiet Pack. The suspension has been lowered 4in at the front and one spline at the rear, KYB shocks being used all round. One-piece door windows have been added, and the whole car sprayed alpine white, set off by polished five-spoke wheels. US-specification lights with Porsche lenses are used at the front, and blue dots at the rear. Inside, the seats have been trimmed in gray velour.

Mark Salisbury owns one of the most radical VW roadsters in the UK. Based on a '73 sedan that originally cost next to nothing, it took two years to complete, much of that time being spent on the body. First, suicide doors were installed, then the roof was chopped, the lights frenched, all the chrome removed, the door tops rolled and a full roll cage built in. Paint is blue pearl mica overlaid with multi-colored graphics. The rear seat has been removed completely, and the fronts replaced with Recaros. The 1776cc engine has big-valve heads and a Turbo Terror exhaust. BBS-style wheels finish the package.

'Dust and Bones' is the nickname of Iain Johnstone's Baja Bug, which is appropriate considering his profession: he's a mortician. Built over a 12-month period, the car has a chopped top, bobbed fenders and graphic paint. Other features include frenched rear lights, one-piece door windows, billet mirrors and color coded headlight rings. The 1600cc engine features twin Kadron carbs with polished aluminum intakes. The rear end has been raised 4in and is fully detailed, while the front runs disc brakes and Sway-Away adjusters.

Steve Kay's radical '72 Beetle roadster took the UK scene by storm on its début, and it has been collecting trophies ever since. Steve had always wanted a roadster and, being a panel beater by trade, figured his talents would cope with a full-on attempt at a show-winning car. He started work in 1991, replacing the whole bottom half of the car because it was rotten. The amount of work that has gone into this car is quite staggering: it took three months alone to get the suicide doors right. It was worth it, however, as his roadster has been voted Europe's Most Beautiful Beetle.

While on a tour of duty in America, in 1965, a British soldier by the name of Blackwell bought a Deluxe Beetle. In 1977 he was posted to America again and took the car with him. Then, in 1985, he retired from the army and returned to England where, sadly, he died a few years later. The car was left to his son who, in 1992, moved to Hong Kong, but before he went, he sold the car to James Roper. James has left the Bug pretty much as it's always been, including the six-volt electrics, although he has added EMPI-style wheels and an EMPI glove box handle.

Mads Moller Nielsen comes from Denmark, where his very clean Cal-look Bug turns heads wherever it goes. Finished in a ferocious shade of yellow, this Bug rolled out of Wolfsburg in 1960. Little is known of what happened to it between 1960 and when it fell into Nielsen's hands, but it certainly looks the business now. Retaining its original 1200cc engine, the car features lowered suspension, while the floorpan has been blasted clean and painted black. Tinted one-piece door windows were fitted, along with EMPI wheels all round. Front lights are US-specification, while the rears are original. Inside, Ford Escort XR3i seats have been fitted in the front, the original rear seat having been reupholstered. A Kenwood CD player provides the entertainment.

Where custom Beetles are concerned, engines come in all shapes and sizes. And in almost all cases, they are finished to spotless perfection, with chromed, polished and painted surfaces providing some of the most awesome engine bays you are ever likely to see. When faced with perfection like this, all you can do is take a step back and simply admire the incredible amount of work and imagination that goes into building such beautiful machines. And whether they are street, show or race engines, the attention to detail is mind numbing. It is almost impossible to think of any other kind of car that commands this level of skill and dedication, and produces such an amazing array of engine styles.

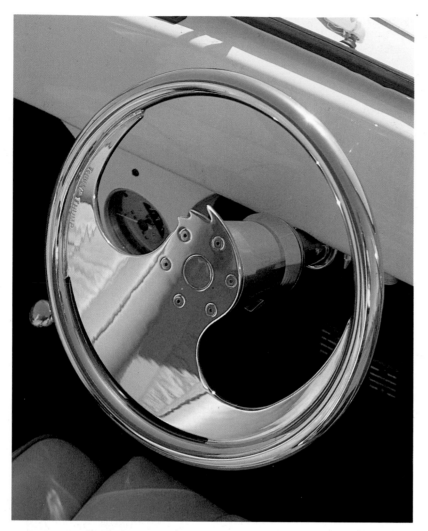

'Lemon Bavois' is owned by Darren Peat, and is one of Britain's leading show cars. Darren's Bug started life in 1967 and underwent a full restoration before he decided to take a more radical approach. Running a stock 1600cc engine with twin baby Dellortos, the car has been lowered front and back, and has been fitted with disc brakes at the front. Bodywork is extensive, and includes a targa top and rolled rocker panels, while the paint is a custom lemon mix. 'Lemon Bavois' still has its original floorpan, which has been cleaned and painted, and rolls on Porsche wheels. The interior has been elegantly trimmed in gray leather and features Recaro front seats - the original remains in the rear. A ten-disc Kenwood CD autochanger provides entertainment on long road trips.

Here are three great drag strip Bugs. 'Clockwork Orange' is owned by Cliff Watkins and uses its original floorpan, although the body has been channeled. With its 1265cc flat-four, the car has run a best quarter mile time of 10.70 seconds. The John Maher car features a full tube frame and, once again, a 1265cc motor. Its best time so far is 10.95 for the quarter. This Bug was the first, outside the States, to run in the tens with a non-turbo, non-nitrous engine.

From the US comes the So Cal Imports car, which features all the latest tube-frame technology.

This highly-accessorized Bug is owned by Sharon Stevens and Dave Foster, who carried out most of the work on it themselves. Very much in the resto-Cal style, this '77 really does look the part. It features pre-'67 wings, US-specification head-lights, louvered running boards, peep mirrors, US tail rails and a fiberglass hood. Paint is Fiat Uno green, while the interior has been finished in contrasting two-tone cream vinyl. An early dashboard has been fitted, along with an early fuel gauge and speedometer, cream switch gear and a wood-rimmed steering wheel. Sharon and Dave retained the original '77 1200cc engine.

Andrew King spent three and a half years building his car. The body was removed and bare-metalled, most of the panels requiring some sort of repair. An early front valance was fitted, together with a pre-'67 hood. The front bumper was swapped for a blade type, while pre-'67 fenders with sloping US-specification headlights were fitted. An early decklid was also added with Popes' Nose light. This car combines the classic Cal-look and high-tech trickery, thanks to the subtle use of billet aluminum and Ford RS2000 wheels. The amethyst metallic paint maintains the contemporary theme; inside black and grey upholstery works well with Porsche high-back seats.

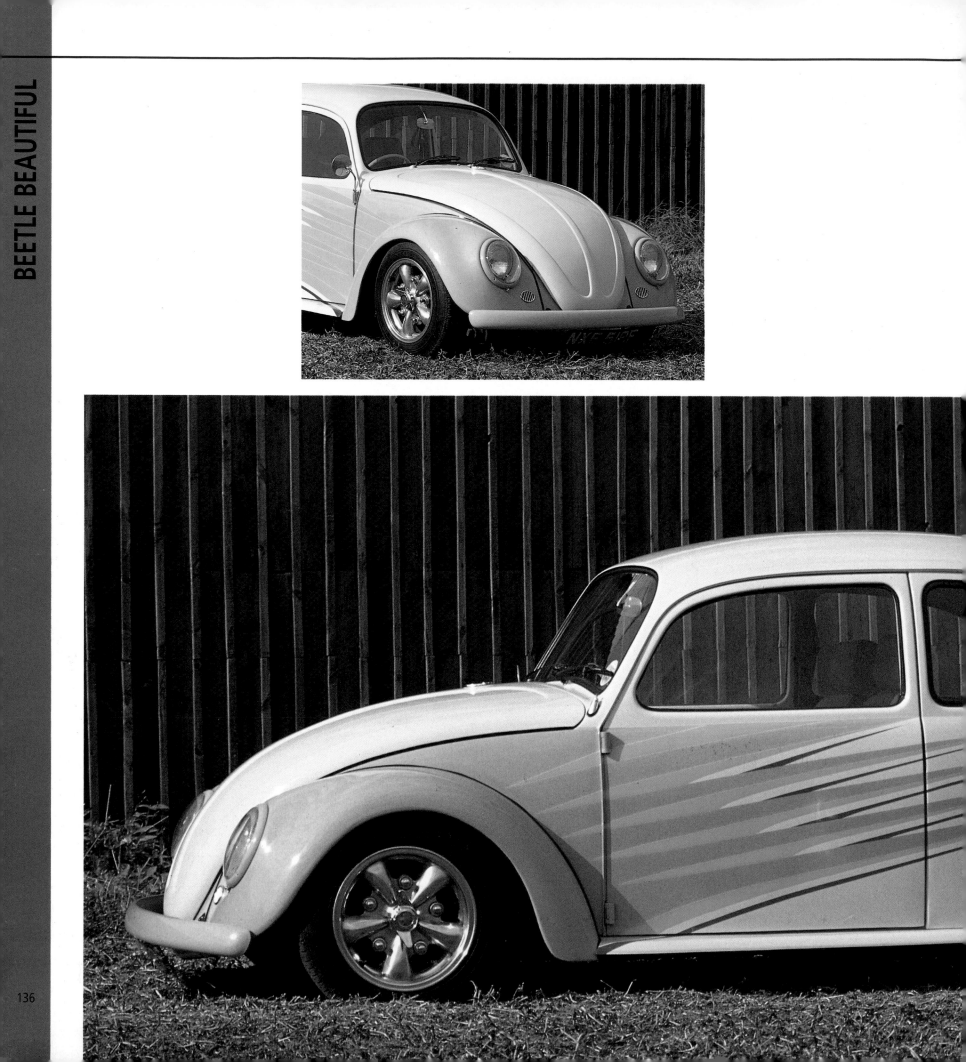

You can't help but notice the paint on David Heading's '67 Type 1 - it smacks you right between the eyes. David was given the Bug for his 16th birthday. He stripped the car himself and resprayed it Peugeot turquoise. After a couple of years, he stripped it again, dechromed the body, and fitted new front fenders and solenoid door latches. This time, it was sprayed peach and green, and kitted out with EMPI wheels. The fenders were shaved and the suspension lowered. Inside, David fitted Dee sports seats and door panels. The 1300cc Type 1 engine is basically stock, but is equipped with a Bug Pack manifold and Turbo Trip silencer.

CONCEPT 1
& THE FUTURE

Legendary is a much over-used term, but where the Beetle is concerned it is entirely appropriate. Among its devotees, the Beetle exercises a hold that is difficult to explain; it is a compulsive machine that gets under people's skin.

While this certainly applies to the millions of Beetle enthusiasts around the world, it is surprising to discover that Volkswagen itself has not forgotten the Bug. At the 1994 Detroit Motor Show, VW stole the limelight from every other major manufacturer with a prototype called Concept 1. VW claimed that, as the name suggested, it was simply a concept car, but the bulbous wings and aerodynamic panels fooled no one: Concept 1 is a Beetle for the nineties.

Right: Protestations from VW about Concept 1 being just another concept car fooled no one. This Beetle for the nineties shoulders a heavy responsibility in carrying the Beetle legend toward a new millennium. While it is very likely that Concept 1 will not be called Beetle when it goes into production, all the visual cues point toward Ferdinand Porsche's original.

APPROPRIATELY ENOUGH, Concept 1 was conceived in the birthplace of the hot Beetle - California - where VW has a design studio. So far, two versions of the car have been built, a sedan and a cabrio, both of which have received much public acclaim.

Outwardly, Concept 1 certainly owes much to the Beetle, and while the new car has a nineties feel, it still manages to retain the sense of quirkiness that gave the Beetle its personality. However, while the exterior of the car pays homage to the original Beetle, underneath things are very different. Gone are the fixtures and fittings of yesteryear: Concept 1 features all the elements of a modern car, including air conditioning, automatic transmission, radio-cassette with compact disc player, twin airbags, side impact bars and ABS. The new car is also shorter and wider than the original Bug, but it has a longer wheelbase.

However, it is in the engine department that Concept 1 strays most obviously from the ideals of the original Beetle. Modern technology means that it is no longer necessary to mount the engine at the rear for maximum interior space. Thus, Concept 1 has a front-mounted engine. Moreover, three different powerplants have been tried, and not one of them is air-cooled.

Volkswagen is keen that Concept 1 should be fuel efficient and environmentally friendly. To this end, the car has been equipped with one of its four-cylinder, turbocharged, direct-injection TDI engines linked to an Ecomatic semi-automatic transmission. Of course purists will say that this takes the Concept 1 too far from the original idea of the Bug and would argue that it should not be called the Beetle for the nineties. However, it could be argued that with this new design the company is perpetuating the Beetle's long tradition of innovation.

Concepts 1's Ecomatic transmission system is a good example of such innovation. The Ecomatic works on the same principle as a bicycle, as it uses power only when it needs it. When Concept 1 is stationary, say at a road junction, the engine is automatically switched off. Yet, when it is time to move off again, a blip of the accelerator restarts the car. VW has run tests with this system and has found it to be 25 per cent more efficient than a standard diesel set-up. The company is also considering using an electric motor in Concept 1.

Like the Beetle, the Concept 1 has been designed as a family car and can carry four people. However, the slick, modern shape means that headroom in the rear is more restricted than in the Beetle.

In reality, Concept 1 will never succeed the Beetle - in fact, if you were looking for a successor to the Bug, it would have to be the Golf. However, what Concept 1 does have in common with the Beetle is its styling: the

bulbous fenders, single-dial dash and retro-feel all echo the Beetle. So strong is the Bug's influence over the design that not even the modern 18in wheels and high-tech gadgets can detract from it.

Concept 1 also carries on the unique feel of the Bug, by swimming against the tide of modern car design. Most of the major manufacturers are currently building production and concept cars that either look like jelly moulds or misshapen eggs. VW's Concept 1 comes as a breath of fresh air and in no way resembles anything else currently being produced. For this, VW should be congratulated. Concept 1 also has that 'almost human' feel that was so much part of the Beetle's make-up, and it looks like it could be a lot of fun to drive. Despite these similarities, however, it seems unlikely that Concept 1 will be named after the Beetle, if and when it finally goes into production and on to the road.

And therein lies the pertinent question: will Concept 1 ever make it into the showrooms? The word from VW is that it *will* be built and will go on sale in 1998. Both the sedan and the cabrio are set to enter production, but are unlikely to look exactly like the original Concept 1. The odds are that some of the more conceptual elements will be removed, and items such as the 18in wheels will not make the final versions in an effort to keep costs down.

Far left, left and above: So far, Concept 1 has been produced as a sedan and cabrio. While the body features many of the rounded, bulbous surfaces of the original Bug, underneath things have changed drastically. For a start, the engine is at the front, and it is no longer air-cooled. In addition, there are all the modern gizmos you would expect of any nineties car, including air conditioning, radio-cassette with CD player, twin airbags, side impact bars and ABS. VW is also keen that the new car be environmentally friendly, and to this end has fitted a four-cylinder, direct-injection TDI engine, running through a special semi-automatic transmission. While none of this bears any relation to the original Bug, Concept 1 still maintains an air of fun and originality, tinged with a quirkiness that always made the Beetle something special.

A

ABS 140, 141
airbags 140, 141
air conditioner 85
air conditioning 140, 141
Armstrong shocks 23
autobahns 8, 10
Autocraft Engine 99
automatic transmission 99, 102,
  140

B

Baja Bug 92, 93, 102, 109, 119
  peninsula 92
  racing 82
Bambus parcel shelf 53
BBS-style wheels 116
Becker quick-release radio 55
Beetle Beautiful 90-137
Billabug clothing company 88
Blaupunkt radio 23

BMW 42
Bosch spotlights 39
braking parachute 94, 113
Bug Pack manifold 137

C

cab 85
Cal-look 64, 69, 77, 85, 86, 88,
  92, 93, 97, 100, 105, 109, 110,
  124, 134
Cal scene 16
Cal style 115
cd 12
Concept 1 138-141
Coupe 27
Creative Car Craft 99
custom scene 16

D

Daimler-Benz 10, 12
Dee sports seats 137

door panels 137
Dehne fuel gauge 53, 61
Dellorto carburetors 97, 105,
  115, 128
Der Kleiner Panzers 92
Detroit Motor Show 138
drag racing 90, 92, 94, 113, 131

E

Eagle 520 wheels 100
Eberspacher gas heater 55
Ecomatic transmission 140
Eliminator heads 107
EMPI 41, 71, 90, 97, 122, 124,
  137
Eurorace rods 90

F

Ferrari 14, 42, 66
Firebird International Raceway
  102

Ford, Henry 14
Foxcraft fender skirts 61
Fram bypass oil filter 61
funny car 99

G

Golf 140
GRP panels 94

H

Hebmüller 17, 27, 56
Hella dash spotlight 39
  fan 39
Hemi V8 78
Historic Beetle 8-13
Hitler, Adolf 8, 10
hot rods 93
Human Car, The 64-89

J

Jaguar 42

K

Kadron carburetors 23, 100, 119
Karosserie Stoll 27
Kenwood sound system 105, 124, 128
Koni shocks 105
KYB shocks 115

L

Lemmertz beauty rings 61
Lohner, Ludwig 10
Low Riders 93

M

Mahle pistons 90
Model T 14
Moto Meter rally dash 39

N

National Socialist Workers Party 10

NSU 10

O

Okrasa engine 56

P

Paintbox bodyshop 110
Petri steering wheel 39
Popes' Nose light 134
Porsche 14
  Ferdinand 8, 10, 12, 138
  high-back seats 134
  lenses 115
  wheels 105, 107, 110, 128
Post Office 55
Pro-Streeters 93
Powerglide 99, 102

Q

Quiet Pack exhaust 23, 97, 100, 115

R

RDA 12
Recaro seats 97, 116, 128
resto-Cal 16, 17, 32, 44, 62, 132
roadster 107, 110, 116, 121
Robri gravel guards 32, 39, 42, 61
  running board step plates 61
roll cage 94, 113
Rolls Royce 66

S

Scat camshaft 90
semi-automatic transmission 141
Sewfine 100
side impact bars 140, 141
Steyr 10
surf scene 64
Sway-Away adjusters 23, 44, 105, 119

T

taxi 85
TDI engine 140, 141
Testarossa side pod kit 107
tube chassis 94, 113
Turbo Terror exhaust 116
Turbo Trip silencer 137

V

Vintage & Restored 14-63

W

Wall Street Crash 10
wheelstands 113
World War 2 12, 16

Y

youth culture 64

Z

Zündapp 10

ACKNOWLEDGMENTS

The publishers are grateful to both individuals and companies who have supplied the photographs included in this book.

© Colin Burnham - 1, 2/3, 4/5, 7, 14/15, 16, 17 left, 18, 19, 24, 25, 26, 33, 56, 57, 62, 63, 64/5, 71 top, 74, 75, 77 right, 78 left, 80 bottom, 82, 83, 86, 87 top, 92, 93 bottom, 94 bottom, 95, 108, 109, 142/3, 144, both endpapers

© Mike Key - cover, 17 right, 20, 21, 22, 23, 30, 31, 32, 34, 35, 36, 37, 38, 39, 44, 45, 46, 47, 48, 49, 50, 51, 52, 53, 54, 55, 58, 59, 60, 61, 96, 97, 98, 99, 100, 101, 104, 105, 114, 115, 116, 117, 122, 123, 124, 125, 128, 129, 136, 137

© Jim Maxwell - 66, 67, 68/9, 70 top, 70/71 bottom, 72, 73, 76/7 left, 78/9 right, 80 top, 81, 84, 85, 87 bottom, 102 bottom, 113 top, 126, 127, 131 top

© Jacky Morel - 88, 89

© Gary Stuart - 90/1, 120, 121

Gary Stuart/© Salamander Books - 93 top, 106, 107, 110, 111, 118, 119, 132, 133, 134, 135

Andy Tipping/© Salamander Books - 27, 28, 29, 40, 41, 42, 43

Courtesy International Vintage Volkswagen magazine - 8/9, 10, 12/3 bottom

Courtesy Volkswagen Publicity - 12 top, 13 right, 138/9, 140, 141

From the archives of Dr. Ing. h.c.F. Porsche, Stuttgart - 11

© Andy Willsheer - 94 top, 102 top, 102/3 right, 112, 113 bottom, 130 top, 130/1 bottom